ALL INDIA

ALL INDIA

Edited by:
Reginald Massey

CONTRIBUTORS:
Marc Alexander
Kailash Budhwar
Balraj Khanna
Reginald Massey
Biman Mullick
Swraj Paul
Eilean Pearcey
Meera Taneja

LEFT: The diversity of stunning wildlife in India matches the diversity of the country's physical geography and extremes of climate.

ABOUT THE CONTRIBUTORS

MEERA TANEJA was born in Delhi and educated in India, Sweden, Burma and Pakistan. Her father, an Indian diplomat, took his family with him whenever he was posted abroad. It is on account of this that from an early age she developed a palate for various cuisines. Later, after a spell of working in Japan, she began writing cookbooks. A trained home economist, she has specialized in communicating her love of Indian food through books, television and radio. In conjunction with a London travel agency she has recently organized the well known "Gourmet Tours of India".

REGINALD MASSEY, poet, novelist, film maker, lecturer, authority on Indian culture, music and dance, is former Editor-in-Chief of *Asian Post International.* He represented India at the first Commonwealth Poetry Conference and is joint author — with his actress wife Jamila Massey — of *The Music of India* and *The Immigrants.* His writings in various publications have helped towards fostering an intelligent appreciation of Asian culture in the West. He wrote and produced *Bangladesh I Love You,* a film starring the boxing phenomenon Muhammad Ali. An MA in Literature, he is a member of the British Academy of Songwriters, Composers and Authors, and is a Fellow of the Royal Society of Arts.

SWRAJ PAUL was one of the moving spirits behind the 1982 Festival of India in the United Kingdom. A mechanical engineer by profession — he has a master's degree with honors from MIT — he now heads an international group of companies headquartered in London. His interests on both sides of the Atlantic encompass hotels, shipping, real estate and steel. He has written *Indira Gandhi* a personal biography of the late Prime Minister of India which was published last year. Among his various awards he numbers the Padma Bhushan — conferred on him by the President of India — as the most precious.

MARC ALEXANDER grew up in Poverty Bay, New Zealand, and worked first as a journalist before devoting himself to traveling and travel-writing. His fascination with India began as a young man when he spent months traveling the country on train, bus and bullock cart. Since then he has visited the subcontinent several times as travel writer and explorer. His latest book is *The Dark Domain,* a novel. Maisie, his late wife, hailed from Lucknow.

KAILASH BUDHWAR, an MA of Allahabad University, is head of the Hindi and Tamil services of the BBC. The Hindi service has 35 million regular listeners in India, and the Tamil audience is scattered between the Middle East and Australia. His broadcasting career started with All India Radio and in 1970 he joined the BBC. In India he was also an actor, having been a member of Prithvi Theaters — the leading company of the Hindi-Urdu stage.

BIMAN MULLICK studied at Calcutta University and St Martin's School of Art in London. He is perhaps best known for his award-winning Gandhi Centenary stamp for the British Post Office, and the first set of eight stamps for the new republic of Bangladesh. As an illustrator and designer he works for leading publishers such as Oxford University Press, Macmillan, and Hamlyn. During the 1982 Festival of India in Britain he designed the *India Today* exhibition held in the Houses of Parliament.

BALRAJ KHANNA studied at Punjab University, Chandigarh. On moving to Europe he became a painter and started exhibiting in Paris, London and New York. Drawing on the springs of his native land he has arrived at a creative *modus* that is essentially meditative although he has affinities with certain European masters and American expressionists. He is now one of his country's leading contemporary painters and has often been compared to Paul Klee. His work is represented in numerous public collections in India, Europe and the United States. His novel *Nation of Fools* (Michael Joseph, London 1984) has been hailed as India's answer to *Catcher in the Rye.* Another novel, *Partition* — set during the partition of India in 1947 — was published last fall.

EILEAN PEARCEY, a graduate of Melbourne University, began her career as a figure and landscape painter after having studied in Paris and London. In 1940 her London studio was bombed and she spent the rest of the war on intelligence work for the Naval Staff in Whitehall. After the war she returned to ballet as a theme, and today is well known for her drawings of dancers in action. Among those who have collected her work are Anton Dolin, Marcel Marceau, Ram Gopal, Alvin Ailey, William Louther, Ritha Devi and Mrinalini Sarabhai. Her drawings have appeared in various international magazines. She is a yoga pupil of BKS Iyengar of Pune and has taught *hatha* yoga.

OPPOSITE: **Shikharas fit for sybarites on Lake Dal in Srinagar, Kashmir. "Shikhar", hunting or shooting, was once one of the favorite pastimes of the local rulers and their guests; Srinagar today is enjoyed still for its moderate climate and fabulous situation rather than the hunting it offers.**

CONTENTS

LEFT: A Hindustan Ambassador, a fluorescent film billboard and part of the fortifications on the old walls of Jaipur are quintessentially Indian images. The Ambassador is still manufactured on an Oxford Morris design of the 1950's; billboards everywhere advertise the lastest products of India's colossal film studios; the city of Jaipur is a monument to the imperial India of the Mughals.

A QUINTET BOOK

Published by Apple Press Ltd
293 Gray's Inn Road
London WC1X 8QF

ISBN 1 85076 050 0

This book was designed and produced by Quintet Publishing Limited, 6 Blundell Street, London N7 9BH

From an original concept by Michael Friedman, Quarto Marketing, New York.

Typeset in Great Britain by QV Typesetting, London. Colour origination in Hong Kong by Universal Colour Scanning Limited, Hong Kong. Printed in Hong Kong by Leefung-Asco Printers Limited.

INTRODUCTION

CULTURAL EXCHANGES

"What this country needs is more agriculture and less culture," was the standing joke when India was going through a series of foodgrain shortages not too long ago. Happily the country has now become self-sufficient in food thanks to the Green Revolution. And those who are responsible for the cultural life of the country can now get on with the job without being laughed at.

No country in the world can offer the cultural variety that India has — from Kashmir in the north to Kanya Kumari in the south; from Kutch in the west to Tripura in the east. Every state in the republic now has its own cultural academy.

This diversity is not only a matter of geography; it is also a matter of scale. India is the foremost example of the ancient living side by side with the very verges of the 21st century. Jetliners streak over a countryside on which bullock-drawn carts with wooden wheels are still common. Buffaloes pull ploughs in the very shadow of nuclear power plants. And modern skyscrapers stand literally side by side with thatched huts that lack running water. The list of paradoxes is endless.

The difference in physical appearance is stunning, as are the differences in dress, language, religion, food, and even gesture.

In India you will meet sober-suited men who speak in the accents of Oxford, yet others might speak English that few foreigners would recognize. In the forests of Madhya Pradesh live aborigines whose way of life has changed little in centuries. Their forefathers were pushed into the inaccessible jungles by Aryan invaders who entered the subcontinent around 2000 BC. The Aryans intermarried with some of the original inhabitants of their new new homeland and called their domains "Aryavarta" — land of the Aryans.

"India" is not an Indian word. Strictly speaking, neither is "Hindu". In none of the ancient, and not so ancient, texts do these words appear. The river Indus which flows through Pakistan was known as "Sindhu" to the Aryans. This was later corrupted by the Persians and Greeks to "Indus"; the people living beyond the "Indus" were called "Hindus", and hence their country became "India". "Aryavarta" and, later, "Bharat" were the two names that the Aryans used for 'their country'. "Bharat", therefore, had connotations of culture rather than of political boundaries. In Hindi, the official national language of India, "Bharat" is the word used. Even this, however, gained recognition only in 1949, when it was written into the constitution, in English.

The next great influence after the Aryan on the subcontinent was that of Islam, which first came to India in the 8th century. The Islamic people were of differing ethnic groups — Arabs, Turks, Persians, Afghans, and Mongols. All brought with them their own contributions to the multi-colored fabric of Indian society. Islamic Sufi thought made a great impact and encouraged the birth and spread of the Bhagti movement which stressed the brotherhood of man.

The Islamic influence on Indian life and culture cannot be underestimated. In today's food, language, dress, and *mores* the Muslim imprint is evident, although it has been Indianized to suit the

ABOVE: Queen Victoria still surveys the capital of the Raj, but Calcutta's skyline is very different from when she reigned, symbolizing the enormous leaps in India's commercial and technological advances since independence. India has developed her own sophisticated hi-tec industries and is no longer content with purchasing Western technology.

genius of the people. The baggy cotton trousers (*shelvars*) so popular in north India were introduced by the Muslims. Similarly the long coat for men (*shervani* or *achhkan*) was originally a Muslim garment. Hindi has absorbed many Persian and even Arabic words. The seclusion of women, another Muslim practice, was adopted by upper-class Hindus. In architecture, the Muslims brought the dome and the arch to India.

The third significant input into India's culture is that which came with British rule. It meant the introduction of the English language, British ideas of education, Protestant ethics, industry, capitalism and technology. The philosopher Radhakrishnan, who became President of India, once remarked that India was indebted to England for three great boons: Shakespeare, the Authorized Version of the Bible, and the limited liability company.

India has indeed absorbed many influences.

AMERICANS — INDIANS

The Indian community in the United States is not a large one, but what they lack in numbers they make up in quality. They are, by and large, highly-trained professionals — doctors, dentists, engineers, computer experts, and academics. India can justly be proud of her progeny for they are contributing to the professional life of many American cities. They are also a vital element of the marvelous kaleidoscope that constitutes American culture.

A few Indians found their way to north America two or three generations ago. They settled on the west coast in British Columbia and California and have done enormously well. Later, many students came either by their own efforts or via educational programs such as the Fulbright scheme.

The first culture shock hits young Indians on the very first day on campus. There seems to be an unbridgable difference between American and Indian university life. In India the student is accustomed to the formality of a disciplined college, whereas in America informality is the norm. The young Indian soon realizes that learning is not a matter of formal instruction. If he is alert he will benefit from the first-class teaching and the practical exposure to engineering that prevails in centers of excellence such as the Massachusetts Institute of Technology.

Professor Paul Samuelson has stated: "The worst bottlenecks are always at the top". If only the leaders and media men could see that India and the United States must start understanding each other

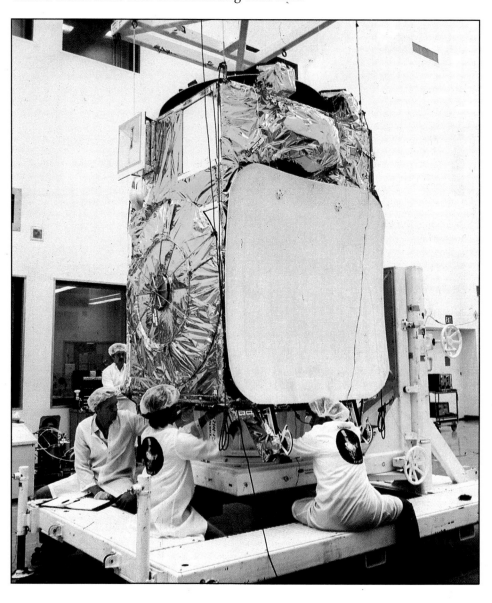

BELOW: The educational system for the subcontinent's rural schools will rely increasingly upon satellites like the Insat 1B, the Indian national satellite which was launched in August 1983.

ABOVE: *The mighty steel structure of Calcutta's Howrah bridge. The dhows carrying merchandise up and down river will no doubt survive far into the future whatever the pace of technological development.*

driest deserts. Both too are richly blessed with fertile plains, great rivers, and still untapped resources of energy and minerals. Geography has also prescribed that the two countries share in common the vagaries of a glorious, if rigorous, climate. India — as the tourists are increasingly discovering — enjoys sea, sand and sunshine to rival that of Florida. But it also suffers, as does the mid-west, from tornadoes, blizzards and heatwaves.

History ensured that both countries should wrest their freedom from the British. As a result they share many of the values and institutions that were inherited, in common, from the British. These include a commitment to the ballot box rather than to the bullet, and an equal devotion to an independent judiciary based on a legal system that reaches back to the Magna Carta. The two nations also share something close to a common language, though you might not recognize it as such when listening to the accents of Chicago and Calcutta. Neither of them uses the Queen's English. There are other, even more relevant, characteristics that India and the United States share.

Within each country there are wide regional differences in terms of ethnic stock, religion and background. Betweeen the Hispanic Americans of the south west or the newly arrived Amer-Asians and the Yankees of New England there are differences no less profound than those that distinguish Bengali, Punjabi or Tamil. This "similarity of dissimilars" is however underwritten by a remarkable human congruence — both peoples share a warmth in human relations and a tradition of large-hearted hospitality.

The constitutional rights and identities of the constituent states of both India and the USA are rooted in similar arrangements. They have separate elected assemblies and separate governors (or chief ministers) and each state has its own special characteristics with the will to uphold them.

The federal system reflects the size and diversity of the two countries. Indeed, *"E Pluribus Unum"* applies just as well to the Union of India as it does to the United States of America.

better. The time has now arrived for a massive effort of rediscovery. In principle, of course, Americans and Indians are remarkably well placed to do this. History and geography have combined to endow both with important common characteristics.

Both India and the United States are large — stretching, as the American anthem says, "from sea to shining sea". America the Beautiful shares with India some of the world's highest mountains and

IMAGES OF FAITH

TOP LEFT: *A brahmin sitting on the ghats at Varanasi after his ritual bath; he is annointing himself in readiness for prayers or* puja.

BOTTOM LEFT: *Nanak was the first Sikh guru. The Sikh national holy day is centered around him.*

TOP RIGHT: *Gobind Singh, the tenth guru, proved that Sikhs were a force to be reckoned with. He created the idea of a Sikh state which reached from Amritsar in the east to the Khyber Pass in the west and from Tibet in the north to the Arabian Sea in the south.*

BOTTOM RIGHT: *The priest is reading from the* Granth Sahib *the Sikhs' holy book which combines the works of the ten Sikh gurus with a blend of Hindu and Islamic texts.*

THE LIVING GODS

In India there is no legend or mythology, for they are so *alive* in the daily existence of the ordinary people that they are, indeed, a part of life itself. Krishna and Rama appear in the two epics, the *Mahabharata* and the *Ramayana*. The variations of their names and the epithets applied to each are legion and millions of men and women have taken these names as their own.

The gods of Hinduism were at once super-human and human and there was a feeling of warmth and even familiarity toward them. The greatest lesson of the epics is the final triumph of a kind of cosmic justice or balance. Even an illiterate peasant will tell you that what he sees round him is a *lila,* a play, and that at a point in the cycle of time all will be ordered and well.

The popular image of Krishna is that of a god who sported on the banks of the Yamuna river and who broke the heart of many an almond-eyed maiden. But Krishna had a more serious side to his character, which can only be appreciated with a full reading of the *Mahabharata*. The stirring verses tell the story of the dynastic struggle between the Kauravs and the Pandavs who were close cousins

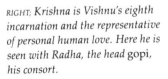

RIGHT: Krishna is Vishnu's eighth incarnation and the representative of personal human love. Here he is seen with Radha, the head gopi, his consort.

The epic is believed to have a basis in history, the events supposedly occurring between 1400 and 1000 BC. As time passed the facts were embroidered upon as so often happens in oral traditions. In *c.* AD 400 the poet Vyas compiled and perhaps even added to the existing material. What we have now is a didactic work that lays down codes of conduct or *dharma.*

Krishna served as the charioteer of Arjun one of the Pandavs. On the battlefield of Kurukshetra, north of Delhi, Arjun hesitated, for he could not happily slaughter his own family. He asked Krishna's advice and the god's advice to him has come to be known as the *Bhagavad Gita.* This poem is, to a large extent, the very foundation of what might be called the Hindu religion.

The Pandavs won eventually, although Krishna was accidentally killed by an arrow which hit his only vulnerable spot — his left heel.

Apart from the *Gita* and the Kaurav-Pandav contest, the epic has romance in the immortal love of Nala and Damayanti and Savitiri's legendary devotion to the memory of her dead husband, which makes her the prototypal Indian wife.

Another model woman is Sita, wife of the man-god Rama and hero of the second epic, the *Ramayana* written by Valmiki in c. 300 BC.

Rama represented qualities such as honor, courage and valor and is held up as a model of manliness.

Sita was carried off one day by Ravana, the brilliant but evil king of Lanka. On learning of Ravana's perfidy, Rama invaded Lanka with the help of Hanuman's monkey army.

The *Mahabharata* and *Ramayana* are known in countries far beyond the borders of India and there are many dance dramas that re-enact episodes from the two epics. They preserve, as it were, the race memory of the Indian people.

In traditional Hindu homes girls are brought up to be Sitas and Savitiris and boys are instructed to emulate the high-minded Rama — resolute in adversity, brave in battle and forgiving in victory.

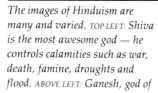

The images of Hinduism are many and varied. TOP LEFT: *Shiva is the most awesome god — he controls calamities such as war, death, famine, droughts and flood.* ABOVE LEFT: *Ganesh, god of wisdom and prosperity, was decapitated by his father, Shiva due to a misunderstanding, and was revived but had to assume the appearance of the first living animal that he saw, an elephant.*

TOP RIGHT: *Hanuman, the monkey god, Rama's faithful general, is often shown as the guardian of forts, palaces and temples.* ABOVE: *Sherawali Mata is yet another form of Parvati or Durga, Shiva's wife, and has her own festival.*

VILLAGE LIFE

BELOW: This barber in an Udaipur street in Rajasthan is part of a familiar and timeless scene made all the more interesting by the colorful wall painting behind. The barber, probably unable to afford premises of his own, will simply ply his trade on the streets.

RIGHT: 25 miles into the Thar desert from Jaisalmeer the remote Rajasthani village of Khuri maintains contact with the outside world only by post. In the heat of the afternoon the postal clerk clears the mail box and retreats back into the cool of his office. The delightful painted patterns which are common to this region need repainting every time the houses are given a fresh coat of mud.

ABOVE LEFT: An old lady washing pots in Jaipur. From youth until old age every member in an Indian family is alloted a task. The youngest will be watched over by elder brothers and sisters who will also tend the chickens, goats and cattle. The older people attend to domestic chores like this lady.
ABOVE RIGHT: Roopsi village in Jaisalmeer district with grandfather Misnruca and his son and grandchildren in their simple mud-walled home. Rajasthanis are full of hospitality and radiate a sense of happiness despite the hardships of making a living in this arid and harsh desert region.
LEFT: The mother of the Misnruca family is mixing flour and water to make chapatis in her kitchen.

RIGHT: *This village girl from Roopsi is wearing the famous Rajasthan silver and gem studded jewelry. The young girls adorn themselves with the family heirlooms as part of their everyday wear. A familiar sight in the villages are traveling bangle sellers. Most of the women cannot resist the temptation of adding another to their collection.*

THE ART OF EXTERIOR DECORATION

BELOW LEFT: *A stunning example of Kulu valley doorway decoration with a fair-skinned Manali village woman. These women wear their thick woven wrap-around blankets like pinafores.*

BOTTOM LEFT: *A Sikh artisan adds highlights to a window frame decoration at the Golden Temple at Amritsar. The Sikhs have emigrated all over the world, but retain their cultural and religious traditions.*

BELOW RIGHT: *Painted door panels in Udaipur, Rajasthan. Each region in Rajasthan has a particular style of panel decoration. Simple line patterns adorn village houses. Painted lions, tigers and oxen protect the entrances to temples and smart town houses, and fine murals cover palace walls. This stylized scene from an Indian miniature has been used to amusing effect on this doorway.*

LEFT: *In Dhungri village, Kulu valley in northern Himachal Pradesh the daughter of Dhani Ram paints decorative patterns around the doorway of her home with her fingers. This tradition proceeds a big* puja *and has to be completed prior to the festivities. This form of finger painting has been handed down to successive generations.*

LEVELS OF POLITENESS

RIGHT: *The key elements in the daily order of Indian life are the upholding of tradition and respect for position. During the wedding ceremony the women of the bride's family serve the groom who has pride of place.*
BELOW: *Temple offerings are blessed before being distributed to the worshippers.*

Considerations of age and social status play a significant role in conventions of behavior throughout the Indian subcontinent. A man does not have to sport a flowing white beard in order to command respect; all he has to make known is the fact that he is somewhat older than anyone else present. And then — though he might not be considered a "father" — he can certainly behave like and be treated like an "elder brother". Touching the feet of one's parents and elders is still a common occurrence. This of course is not performed by the young as an unpleasant duty. On the contrary, it is a method by which the young earn the blessings of their seniors.

Pointing one's feet at another person is considered very rude; so is sitting in such a manner that the soles of your shoes face another person. Shoes are considered unclean and are removed on entering traditional homes and kitchens. They are also removed when visiting temples, mosques, mausoleums, tombs, and other sacred places.

There are absolute patterns of speech and behavior to fit the company of equals, great friends, mere acquaintances, social inferiors or social superiors. The word "you" has many variations and forms in India — it all depends on who is addressing whom.

Foreigners very often might get the impression that Indians are unnecessarily fawning and obsequious. That is not quite so. Indians are courteous and reluctant to say "No" , particularly to guests, visitors and foreigners.

You might find this exasperating, since you are

in the habit of hearing "Yes" and "No". However, once you realize that the innate politeness of the Indian will not permit him or her to be brutally frank with you, then (and only then) will you begin to enjoy your sojourn. It takes years, however, to appreciate the subtle nuances and hints inherent in the term *ishara*.

Personal hygiene has a high premium — Hindus bathe before temple worship and attached to mosques are washrooms where Muslims carry out their ablutions according to a set ritual. Hands are thoroughly washed before meals: and hands *and* mouths are washed after meals. The right hand is used for all "clean" tasks — such as eating; the left is used for purposes of personal hygiene. Hence when food or gifts are handed to friends the left hand is never used on its own. Either the right is used on its own, or if both are used the left is always *under* the right.

In Muslim areas — such as Kashmir and certain districts of Uttar Pradesh — and in cities with a strong Islamic influence, such as Lucknow and Hyderabad, there is a distinctive social style. Lucknow is famous for its conventions of courtesy, sometimes carried to extreme lengths as the following example will illustrate. Two gentlemen wishing to board the same first-class railway compartment started bowing to each other with a series of "*pehlae aaps*" ("After you, Sir" — "After you, Sir"). Neither moved — but while they were busy being courteous to each other the train whistled and steamed away. The only two left on the platform were the cultured pair. But the story does not end there. They now had an argument; not blaming each other, but each blaming himself for the missed train.

The Lucknow episode is obviously apocryphal, but it gives an indication of the *politesse* that one might encounter in India.

ABOVE: *The most common form of Hindu welcome is namaskar, spoken as the palms are brought together and the head inclined. To respond with* namaskar *confers feelings of special respect and recognition of personal status.*
LEFT: *This young peasant girl outside Badal Vilas Palace, the home of Jaisalmeer's maharaja, highlights the stark gulf between life at the simplest level and palace opulence. She has just collected dung from the palace byre.*

THE ELEPHANT STORY

BELOW: *The elephant has been venerated since ancient times. In areas where the pace of life is slow it is still a cheap and viable alternative to motorized haulage.*
RIGHT: *There are several co-operative schools of art in Udaipur whose objective is to retain the techniques of miniature painting and fine copies of elephants can be found on silk or ivory.*
FAR RIGHT: *On "Arjuna's Penance" stone near Madras the elephants appear in sculptural relief. They are fresh, realistic and unpretentious.*

OPPOSITE CENTER LEFT: *Elephants are often to be found within temple complexes, such as this one at Kanchipuram, one of the seven sacred cities, in southern India. Apart from the obvious connection with Ganesh it is difficult to understand their function.*
OPPOSITE BELOW LEFT: *Washing an elephant with a piece of pumice stone is a time-consuming occupation, however, there is little else to do between sunrise and sunset — the times when visitors to Corbett National Park are given rides deep into the forest in search of game. There is a strong bond between these majestic animals and their keepers, during the bathing an extraordinary dialogue of strange words and noises can be heard.*
OPPOSITE RIGHT: *These wedding festivities in Jaipur are reminiscent of the fine processions that used to take place during the days of the Raj. Wealthy families vie with one another to secure the services of elephants for the procession of the bridegroom to the bride's home.*

LEFT: *In Udaipur the elephants are one of the main subjects of the wall painters, as can be seen from the walls of the City Palace.*
RIGHT: *Ganesh is one of the most popular gods in India. His fluorescent pink jovial expression is seen on many household walls.*